I hope that this adds to the fun you have with finding wild goodies to eat! These will add even more color to your table!

We love you!

Lois & Bob

EDIBLE
FLOWERS

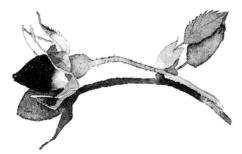

EDIBLE FLOWERS

CLAIRE CLIFTON

ILLUSTRATED
BY

GLYNN
BOYD HARTE

McGRAW-HILL BOOK COMPANY
New York St. Louis
San Francisco Mexico

BY THE SAME AUTHOR
AND ILLUSTRATOR
(with Martina Nicolls)

Edible Gifts

Recipes that have been taken from other sources are
acknowledged in the text. Thanks for permission to use
them are due to the following: p. 20, from *Cuisine of the
Sun: Classic Recipes from Nice and Provence* by Mireille
Johnston. Copyright © 1976 by Mireille Johnston.
Reprinted by permission of Random House Inc; pp. 22
and 50, John Farquharson Ltd; p. 29, Harper and Row
Inc. and Routledge & Kegan Paul Ltd; pp. 32 and 51, The
Medici Society Ltd; p. 54, Jill Norman Ltd; p. 56, J. M.
Dent Ltd; p. 83, Dover Publications Inc.

1 2 3 4 5 6 7 8 9   8 7 6 5 4 3

Library of Congress Cataloging in Publication Data

Clifton, Claire
  Edible Flowers.

1. Cookery (Flowers) I. Title.
Tx814.5.F5C56   1984   641.6   83-18690
ISBN 0-07-011388-2

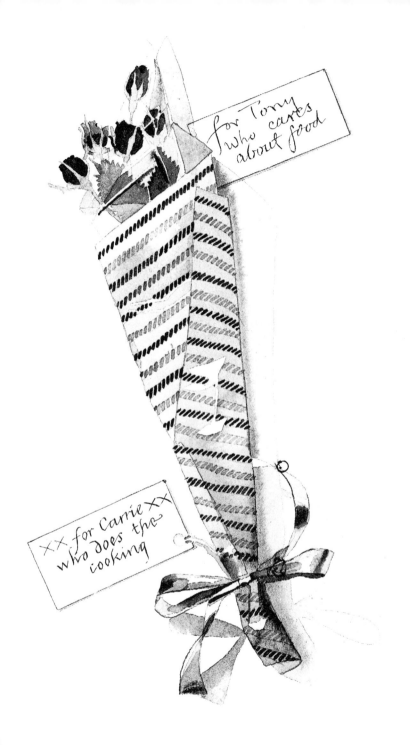

for Tony
who cares about food

xx for Carrie xx
who does the
cooking

CONTENTS

I would like to thank Bamber and Christina Gascoigne for providing most of the edible flowers; Alan Davidson for allowing me to use his library and take up his time; T. A. McKirdy of Cooks Books; Janet Clarke, John Lyle and Jan Longone of The Wine and Food Library for giving me honest advice and finding invaluable books; Gordon Taylor and Guy Cooper of The Herb Society and John Byrne for assistance with research and constant encouragement; my patient friends who ate their way through the experiments; Rebecca Drummond for enthusiastic help with the first rose petal jam; and my parents who let me put cinnamon in the mashed potatoes.

PREFACE

Food made with flowers is not only delicious and beautiful to look at but is also a fascinating link with the past. A delicate pale pink water-ice made with rose petal jam can transport anyone with a little imagination back to a time when a rose cordial could be prescribed 'to wash the mulligrubs out of a moody brain'.

From East to West since ancient times, flowers which we usually think of as purely decorative have been used as food.

Rose water was first mentioned by the poet and doctor Nicander in 140 BC. There are recipes in the classical Roman cookery book of Apicius using roses, mallow flowers, flower bulbs, and for violet and rose wine. All over the Mediterranean today zucchini (courgette) flowers are sold in the summer for cooking, and the popular Italian liqueur Sambuca is flavoured with elder flowers.

Sauce Eglantine, said to have been a particular favourite of Queen Victoria's, was made with wild rose hips from Balmoral. It was a more complicated version of the Saracen Sauce described in the earliest known English cookery book *The Forme of Cury*, compiled by the master cooks of King Richard II around 1390.

Primroses, violets, roses; hawthorn, sloe thorn, and apple blossoms; cowslips, elder, clove-gilly flowers; marigolds, nasturtiums and herb flowers have through the centuries been used for cooking in every conceivable way. They flavoured sugar, sweet sauces, liqueurs and potions; were baked into custards and tarts; pulped into pottages with almonds, sugar and spices; candied, pickled, frittered; made into jams and conserves and were eaten raw in salads. 'Throw nasturtium flowers about the cress' wrote the eighteenth-century writer Hannah Glasse in her directions for a 'Salmagundy'.

In the Orient people are still eating food that would have been familiar a thousand years ago. Even now it is not difficult or even extraordinary to eat or drink something made with flowers every day. In China and Japan tea is mixed with jasmine, roses, lotus, marigolds, narcissus and peonies. Chrysanthemums are fried in batter and, like lily buds and jasmine, are served in soups. In the Middle East roses and orange flowers flavour everything from pastry and ice cream to meat dishes, which are often cooked with dried rose buds.

Part of the charm of flower cookery is its links

with culinary traditions which have their roots in magic, herbal medicine and alchemy. While preparing roses and violets for cooking you could picture yourself pounding them with sugar in the Middle Ages for a delicate child, or in a fragrant still-room in 1600 mixing wild thyme buds with hollyhocks and marigolds for a potion 'To Enable One to See the Fairies'.

All over Europe, insomniacs are still drinking a soothing soporific cup of camomile or lime flower tea before retiring. Carnation is one of the ingredients of the formula for Chartreuse, which is still kept secret by Carthusian monks. Carnation soup was an old remedy for depression. Elder flower champagne, long a country favourite, is the very essence of summer.

Fragile flowers which give so m ᴊh pleasure need not always be 'sweet not lasting. The perfume and suppliance of a minute. No more,' as Shakespeare wrote of violets in *Hamlet*. A sip of hawthorn cordial on a dark winter evening can bring back the hot sunny scent of a summer day.

Eating flowers, which once was common, is never ordinary. 'Think what a poem a salad might be if "dressed" with primrose vinegar,' wrote Florence White. Even though it is no longer possible to buy cowslip 'pips' by the pint, nor would many of us be able to harvest twenty bushels of roses a year for cooking, as the Bishop of Ely did in the sixteenth century from his London gardens, we can still cook with flowers. With this collection of flower recipes I have aimed at bringing this subtle and delicious art within easy reach of anyone who loves flowers and good food.

GATHERING, DRYING
AND STORAGE

Flowers for cooking are not that difficult to obtain.
I have made lavender wine with two dozen heads of
lavender from my window boxes, and always keep
a few scented geranium leaves, grown indoors, in a
jar of sugar. Anyone living in a flat that gets sun can
grow nasturtiums, pinks, scented-leaved geraniums, violets, lavender and marigolds in window
boxes or patio tubs. Old scented roses, lilac,
jasmine and fruit trees are a delicious addition to
even a small town garden. Florists' violets and
mimosa are fine for cooking. In the country or
suburbs anyone may gather hawthorn, elder flower
and wild rose hips. I often cook with dried flowers
and hips which I buy at a herbalists' or a health
food shop.

One of the most important things to remember
about flowers for eating is that they must be
absolutely free from poison. Do not spray insecti-
cide on anything you may want to eat. I have used a
spray of soapy water on pests with varying degrees
of success. The best line of attack may be to try and
get to your flowers before the bugs, birds or rabbits
do. They should be harvested just after blooming
anyway, which may give you the edge. If you buy
dried flowers they will have been grown for
culinary purposes and treated accordingly.

Flowers should be gathered on a dry day when
the morning dew has just dried off the blooms and

they are at their peak of perfection. Usually this is just after blooming, when they are not yet full blown. If you have a choice, pick those that are the furthest away from passing traffic. Exhaust fumes are not an attractive addition to scent and flavour. If you are gathering wild flowers pick only those which are plentiful and be very careful not to uproot the entire plant.

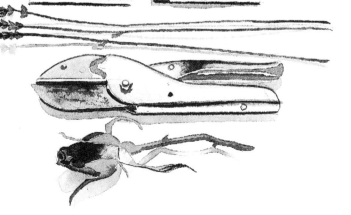

Shake the flowers to eliminate insects; if they are dusty give them a quick rinse under running water, then a shake, and leave them on racks or flat baskets. You can use them while damp but not if they are soggy. They must be dealt with fairly quickly as they wilt rapidly.

Many flowers can be dried for use out of season — rose buds and petals, marigolds, elder, violets, camomile and herb flowers. Pick them when the dew has dried off and spread them out as far apart from each other as possible on screens or wide, flat baskets. The flowers need to have air circulating all around them to dry properly. Place them in the shade and away from breezes, or in an airing cupboard. Shake or stir them around with your hands several times a day until they are completely desiccated and brittle to the touch. Store in cardboard boxes or airtight tins. Make sure they are not even slightly damp when packing them away or they will spoil.

Remove all stems, leaves and green. Cut away the white heels at the base of rose, pink and marigold petals. Small flowers or buds may be left whole.

Not all flowers are edible. Rather than list those which are mildly toxic or deadly, I would strongly suggest that you do not experiment and use only the flowers that are mentioned. If in doubt consult an expert or a reliable reference book.

Many dried flowers, seeds and plants are available by post. To find suppliers look in the telephone directory or contact a herb society.

I
SAVOURY

Flower Vinegars

Flower Butter Sandwiches

Nasturtium Seed Pickles

Pork with Sage, Capers and White Vermouth

Flowers 'La Chiusa'

Eel Soup with Marigolds

Apple, Sage and Marigold Savoury Pudding

Corn and Marigold Pudding

Cold Cherry and Rose Soup

Flower Salads:

Salmon Salad with Violets

Violet Salad

Salad Marie Louise

Watercress, Beetroot and Nasturtium Salad

Nasturtium Salad · Fennel and Mimosa Salad

Elder Flower Pickle

Two Flower Omelettes

Rose Hip Chutney

Pease of the Seedy Buds of Tulips

King's Own Sauce

FLOWER VINEGARS

Vinegar delicately tinted and flavoured with flowers is delicious and very simple to make. Primroses, roses, violets, carnations, elder flowers, nasturtiums, lavender, clover, rosemary or thyme flowers are steeped in good white wine vinegar or cider vinegar for at least two weeks before straining and rebottling the finished product. Make sure the stems, and green and white heels are removed from flowers or petals. With larger flowers, fill a wide-mouthed jar about half or two-thirds full of the flowers, then pour over the vinegar and fill up the jar. Make sure the flowers are completely covered. The blossoms will sink down in a few days and you may add more if you wish. With small flowers you can poke them into the bottle the vinegar comes in without decanting it. A good handful to a pint is about right. If you can leave the jar or bottle in the sun while the flowers are steeping in the vinegar it will help to draw out the flavour of the blooms.

A seventeenth-century recipe 'To Carbonado Beef the Italian Way' calls for rose vinegar, claret wine, elder vinegar and coriander seed to be sprinkled on beef steaks, which should lie on top of each other in a dish for an hour to marinate. Then you grill them, remove the fat from the residue in the pan and, while keeping the meat warm in another dish, boil up the remaining pan juices with the juice of an orange or lemon and a little elder vinegar.

FLOWER BUTTER SANDWICHES

Rose petals, whole violets or clover and sprigs of lilac can be used for this charming old recipe. Just reading it makes me smell summer. Tiny sandwiches spread with flower butter would be delightful for the tea table or on a picnic. You could serve them with a flower tea, elder flower 'champagne' (see page 73) and one of the rose jams from the Sweet section for a tea-time flower feast.

Place a layer of flowers in the bottom of a bowl. Wrap $\frac{1}{4}$ lb of butter in waxed or greaseproof paper and put it on top of the flowers. Sprinkle more flowers over the butter, cover the bowl and leave overnight in a cool place. When you are ready to make your sandwiches, unwrap the butter and spread it on very thin slices of bread. Put two together to make a sandwich with more flowers in between if you like, trim the crusts and cut into triangles to serve. It is a nice touch to decorate the serving plate with flowers as well.

NASTURTIUM SEED PICKLES

Various seeds and buds have been used in the past for pickles, including broom and alexander buds. Nasturtiums were brought to Europe from the New World. They were an instant success and must have made a brilliant show in the gardens of the day. The Elizabethans called them 'yellow lark's heels' and John Parkinson wrote in 1629 that they were 'now familiar in most gardens of any curiosity'. The seed heads should be picked on a dry day, soon after the blossoms are finished. Wash them well and make sure there are no bugs lingering. Leave them to dry in a sieve or spread them on a baking sheet and leave them for 10 minutes in a cool oven. Various eighteenth-century recipes call for grated horseradish, cloves, allspice, ginger, cinnamon, mace, nutmeg and shallots. Some recommend soaking in brine for 3 days but this version is the simplest.

Put enough vinegar to fill the jar you are going to use in a saucepan with a pinch of salt, a few bay leaves and peppercorns. Bring it to the boil and then allow to cool. Pack the dry seeds into the jar and pour the vinegar and seasonings over them. If you like a spicier pickle add some or all of the flavourings mentioned in the paragraph above and boil them up with the vinegar. The pickled heads will be ready to eat in a month and are used in the same way as capers: in salads, sauces for pasta, meat dishes and as a garnish for smoked salmon.

PORK WITH SAGE, CAPERS
AND WHITE VERMOUTH

If you are a messy cook, as I am, a stained page in a cookery book means that the recipe is a great favourite. The page in my copy of Mireille Johnston's *The Cuisine of the Sun* with this one on it is particularly grubby. Instead of capers you could use the pickled nasturtium seeds described on the previous page.

'4 tablespoons olive oil; 3 lbs boneless pork, cut into cubes; 2 onions, chopped; 4 teaspoons chopped fresh sage; 2 bay leaves; 2 tablespoons chopped parsley or fennel leaves; 2 teaspoons thyme; salt and pepper; 1 pint (or enough to just about cover the meat) dry white wine; 1 wine glass dry white vermouth; 4 tablespoons capers.

'Heat the olive oil in a heavy pan. Sauté the pork until browned. Lower the heat and add the onions, herbs, salt and pepper and wine. Cover and cook very slowly for about one and a half hours. Remove the meat and set aside in a warm place. Add the vermouth to the pan. If the sauce is too thin, boil rapidly to reduce. Add the capers and the pork. Cook for a few minutes to reheat the meat, remove the bay leaves and serve in a warm fireproof dish.'

FLOWERS 'LA CHIUSA'

Nancy Jenkins, in whose Tuscan farmhouse I first ate delicious fried zucchini (courgette) flowers, was given this recipe by Dania Luccherini, owner-chef of La Chiusa in Montefollonico. Its advantage over fried flowers is that the cook does not have to stand over a hot stove dodging spattering oil while everyone else is eating, but can prepare most of it in advance, have a glass of chilled white wine while they are cooking, then bring them to the table and sit down with the guests. Any squash flowers will do or even hollyhocks, which are related to the mallow flowers of classical Roman cookery.

You must first make a sauce. Peel, and squeeze the juice and seeds from the finest, freshest tomatoes you can find. Add a little of the best extra virgin olive oil and cook together in a saucepan until you have a fairly thick purée, but do not use any thickening agent of any sort. Set it aside. Then, in a bowl, mix fresh ricotta cheese, a few tablespoons of chopped parsley, a little freshly grated nutmeg, 2–3 tablespoons of freshly grated Parmigiano Reggiano and a beaten egg yolk (1 yolk to every 7–8 flowers). Stir with a fork until it is a stiff paste. Carefully fill each flower with the ricotta mixture. Put the tomato sauce in a shallow fireproof dish and place the filled flowers on top. Cook slowly for about 15 minutes. If the sauce starts to stick add a little water – not broth, you don't want anything to obscure the fresh flavours of the flowers and tomatoes. When they are cooked arrange them on a serving plate or serve them directly from the cooking dish.

EEL SOUP WITH MARIGOLDS

There are a number of eighteenth-century recipes for mutton broth with marigolds but similar nineteenth-century versions inexplicably omit the flowers. Perhaps they just went out of fashion. The marigolds in this soup *circa* 1889 from *Court Favourites* by Elizabeth Craig may be a substitute for more expensive saffron – the stamens of the *Crocus sativus* – which is one of the flavourings of the classic bouillabaisse. Eels are usually available from a good fishmonger.

'Head and tail of a large eel; three quarts of water; 4 oz butter; one leek; blossoms and leaves of 5 marigolds; $\frac{1}{2}$ pint of green peas or asparagus tips; $\frac{1}{2}$ teacup chopped parsley; bunch of thyme; 2 tablespoons flour; 1 pint milk; salt and pepper to taste.

'Put the head and tail in a stewpan with the water, and allow to simmer gently for $2\frac{1}{2}$ hours or more till the fish breaks in pieces when tried with a fork. Strain and pour the liquor back into the pan. Add butter, and when boiling, throw in prepared leek, green peas (or asparagus), parsley, thyme and marigold leaves, all cut up except the bunch of thyme which should be enclosed in a muslin bag. Cover and simmer till vegetables are tender.

'Remove muslin bag. Cream flour with a little of the cold milk, then bring remainder of milk to boiling point with marigold blossoms. Strain, then gradually stir hot milk into the creamed flour. Stir slowly and carefully into the soup to prevent flour lumping. Keep on stirring after the soup comes to the boil for about 5 minutes to remove the rawness from the flour. (Some cooks prefer not to add the parsley till after the soup has come to the boil.) Season with pepper and salt. Arrange slices of toasted bread in the bottom of a tureen. Pour in soup.'

APPLE, SAGE AND MARIGOLD
SAVOURY PUDDING

Apples and sage, traditionally served with pork in one form or another, are combined with the more unusual marigolds in this dish which Dorothy Hartley says comes from Worcestershire and Oxfordshire. She wrote in 1954 that it is 'probably very old'. The original had a shortcrust pastry lining but I prefer a lighter version with the custard filling alone. It is delicious served with roast pork and is cooked in the oven along with the meat. Tart eating apples keep their shape better than cooking apples and are a sharp contrast to the rich meat.

> 2 tablespoons butter; 3 apples, peeled, cored and sliced; ¾ pint milk; 3 eggs; 1 tablespoon chopped fresh sage or a good pinch of dried sage; a few sprigs of thyme or a pinch dried; 1 handful marigold petals, fresh or dried; salt and pepper and a scraping of nutmeg.

These quantities will fill a shallow baking dish 8 inches across and 2 inches deep, and are ample for six servings. Forty minutes before your roast will be done dot the butter in the bottom of the dish, arrange the sliced apples on top of the butter and cook in the oven for about 10 minutes until the apples are just tender. Beat the eggs into the milk, add the seasonings and the flowers and pour over the apples. Put back into the oven and cook with the meat for the last 30 minutes. The custard should be set, lightly browned on the top and puffed up.

CORN AND MARIGOLD
PUDDING

Marigolds give this savoury dish a nice colour, texture and a hint of nuttiness. It can be made more substantial for a light luncheon or as an addition to a vegetarian supper by adding 2 ounces of grated cheese, parmesan or cheddar. I use frozen corn in preference to tinned because it does not have salt or sugar added to it.

1 lb frozen corn kernels; 2 oz butter; $\frac{1}{2}$ pint milk (skimmed is fine); 2 eggs, separated, the whites stiffly beaten; salt and pepper; good handful dried or fresh marigold petals.

Process or mince the corn (or mix it in a blender with the milk). Add the butter, milk, beaten egg yolks, salt, pepper, marigolds, and cheese if you are using it. Fold in the stiffly beaten egg whites and bake in a baking or soufflé dish for 30–35 minutes in a moderate oven (400° F/Gas No. 6). It should be lightly browned on the top and puffed up like a soufflé or quiche.

COLD CHERRY AND ROSE SOUP

When I lived in New York in the 1960s the best restaurants in my neighbourhood were cosy Hungarian establishments where one could eat extremely well for very little money. In the summer cold fruit soups appeared on the menus. They were new to me but I liked them so much I served one at my first grown-up dinner party. The guests, who included my future husband and his best friend, were horrified and thought it most peculiar. I still think fruit soups are delightfully refreshing. This one looks and feels like purple velvet.

1 tin (15 oz) dark pitted cherries with their syrup, or 1 lb fresh cherries, pitted and 3–4 tablespoons sugar (to taste); 1 pint cold water; 1 wine glass red wine; 1 cinnamon stick, broken in half; pinch of freshly grated nutmeg; 1 lemon, thinly sliced (seeds removed); trimmed petals of 1 large or 2 small strongly scented roses (or 2 teaspoons of rose water*); 1 tablespoon cornflour; juice of 1 lemon; sour cream or *fromage blanc*.

Put the cherries, water, red wine, spices, lemon slices and rose petals in a saucepan. Bring to the boil and simmer gently for 15 minutes. Remove the lemon and cinnamon with a slotted spoon. Allow the liquid to cool slightly, then place it in a blender and blend until smooth. Pour it back into the saucepan. Put the cornflour in a small bowl and add enough of the cherry mixture to make a smooth paste. Add the lemon juice and cornflour paste to the liquid in the saucepan. Heat slowly, stirring, until completely blended and very smooth. Add the rose water if you are using it and put the mixture in a bowl to chill in the refrigerator. Swirl a spoonful of sour cream or *fromage blanc* into each bowl when you serve it.

* Rose water used in cooking is distilled and very concentrated. The finest is said to come from Isparta in Turkey where roses are grown for making attar of roses. The Cypriots distil rose water but make sure you buy a brand that is really distilled and not just rose flavoured. Read the label carefully.

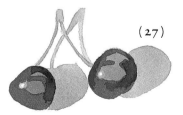

FLOWER SALADS

One of the prettiest ways of eating fresh flowers, and certainly the easiest, is to use them in salads. Here is a selection from various sources.

SALMON SALAD WITH VIOLETS

This is from an 'older book than the 1803 edition of Hannah Glasse'.

'Salette of salmon cut long waies with slices of onions laid upon it and upon that is cast violets, oyle and vinegar.'

Florence White, *Flowers as Food*, 1934

VIOLET SALAD

Mrs Leyel called this a 'delicious dish fit for Lucullus' and M. F. K. Fisher wrote that it was the most exquisite dish she had ever heard of.

'Take a Batavian endive, some finely curled celery, a sprinkling of minced parsley, a single olive, and the petals of a couple of dozen blue violets. These several ingredients are to be mixed with the purest olive oil, salt and pepper being the only condiment. Add a dash of Bordeaux wine and a suspicion of white vinegar.'

Dr W. T. Fernie, *Meals Medicinal*, 1905

SALAD MARIE LOUISE

Alice B. Toklas says, 'The Empress Marie Louise
. . . the last Empress of Russia had a weakness for
violets . . .'

'Take equal parts of sliced boiled cold potatoes and
raw peeled and sliced apples. Add oil, salt and
pepper. Mix at the last moment and place in a
mound in the center of the salad bowl. Sprinkle
with crushed hard-boiled eggs. Surround with
alternate small mounds of corn and of violets,
stems removed.'

Alice B. Toklas, *Aromas and Flavors*, 1958

WATERCRESS, BEETROOT AND
NASTURTIUM SALAD

'Slice the beetroot very thin, and divide the
watercress into sprigs. Take young nasturtium
leaves and arrange the salad in the bowl with walls
of each, placing the beetroot in between the two
greens. Decorate with nasturtium flowers and pour
over the salad a dressing made of nasturtium seeds,
oil, vinegar, salt and pepper.'

Mrs C. F. Leyel, *Picnics for Motorists*, 1936

NASTURTIUM SALAD

'Put a plate of flowers of the nasturtium in a salad bowl, with a tablespoonful of chopped chervil; sprinkle over with your fingers half a teaspoonful of salt, two or three tablespoonsful of olive oil, and the juice of a lemon; turn the salad in the bowl with a spoon and fork until well mixed, and serve.'

Turabi Efendi, *Turkish Cookery Book*, 1864

FENNEL AND MIMOSA SALAD

Miriam Yarrien says this is served in Tunisia. It can be made in the winter with imported mimosa.

Slice the fennel and make a dressing with the best oil and vinegar you have. Almond, walnut or hazelnut oil with fruit or flower vinegar is especially good. Mix the fennel with the dressing and then sprinkle over mimosa blossoms pulled off their stems. Do not mix the flowers with the dressed fennel or they will become soggy.

ELDER FLOWER PICKLE

Flowers were often pickled with sugar and vinegar to be used as an ornament for salads (a layer of flowers or buds, with a layer of sugar to fill a jar, then covered with vinegar). This one is more like a chutney. It comes from a charming wartime pamphlet published by the Medici Society in 1942 called *Wild Fruits, Berries, Nuts and Flowers* which says it is 'very nice with tender cold meat'.

'Gather elder flowers just as they begin to open. Fully open flowers soon lose pollen and flavour. They must be quite dry. Pack them in jars. Cover with boiling white wine vinegar. Cover well. Leave fourteen days before using.'

(32)

TWO FLOWER OMELETTES

X. Marcel Boulestin wrote in *Simple French Cooking for English Homes* in 1923 that his 'Omelette aux Fleurs de Salsifis' isn't easy to make – not because it is difficult to do it well but because it is hard to find the flowers – they aren't in shops but are only to be found in vegetable gardens in the late spring. He says to 'nip them literally in the bud', and wash them well to get rid of the milky liquid which oozes out when you break them. Dry them gently in a cloth and then cook the clean, dry flowers in butter until they are brown. The heat 'affects them more quickly than the sun; some show a few already yellow petals. It is a pretty sight; also the taste is delicious'. Mix the cooked salsify buds with beaten eggs and make your omelette in the usual way.

'Sister Abigail's Blue Flower Omelet' is said to be an old American Shaker recipe in which chive or wild garlic flowers (or crushed nasturtium seeds) are added to a mixture of beaten eggs and milk in the proportion of 12 blossoms to 4 eggs and 4 tablespoonfuls of milk and cooked as you would an ordinary omelette.

ROSE HIP CHUTNEY

Rose hips need not always be gathered from garden or hedgerow. I have made this dark, spicy chutney with a German brand of dried hips which come in 50 gram packets (3 packets make half a pint). It goes very well with ham, game or turkey and is nice to have on hand for the winter holidays.

½ pint dried rose hips or 1 pint fresh hips, seeds removed; 1 pint cider vinegar or wine vinegar; ½ lb raisins or sultanas, chopped; 1½ lbs cooking apples, peeled, cored and chopped; 2 heaped teaspoons ground ginger; 1 rounded teaspoon cayenne pepper; 1 teaspoon ground cloves; 1 large or 2 small cloves garlic, minced; ½ lb brown sugar; juice of 1 lemon.

Soak the rose hips and fruit in the vinegar overnight. Then place with all of the other ingredients in a large, heavy saucepan. Bring to the boil over a high heat, reduce the heat and simmer, stirring occasionally, until the mixture is nice and thick. Leave until cool, then put into clean, dry jars and cover with waxed discs and cellophane and plastic-lined lids, or use a glass jar with a hinged lid and a rubber seal. Store in a cool place. Like all chutneys it improves with age. Keep for at least a month before using.

PEASE OF THE SEEDY BUDS
OF TULIPS

The gifted and handsome Cavalier, Sir Kenelm Digby, confidant of Queen Henrietta Maria, friend of Bacon, Galileo, Descartes, Harvey, Ben Jonson and Cromwell, gives this recipe in *The Closet of the Eminently Learned Sir Kenelme Digbie Kt Opened* published by his son in 1669, four years after his death. Its charm would be lost in translation.

'In the Spring (about the beginning of May) the flowry-leaves of Tulips do fall away, and there remains within them the end of the stalk, which in time will turn to seed. Take that seedy end (then very tender) and pick from it the little excrescencies about it, and cut it into short pieces, and boil them and dress them as you would do Pease; and they will taste like Pease and be very savoury.'

KING'S OWN SAUCE

Almost every old cookery book of any size will have more than a dozen recipes for savoury sauces. Many were named after their creators; Dr Redgill's Sauce Piquant, The Old Admiral's Sauce, Gubbins', Harvey's *et al.* May Byron does not say why this is called 'King's Own' but it is a more stirring name than just plain 'Nasturtium Sauce', as it often appears. Use it as you would Worcestershire sauce on hot or cold meat or splash it in soup or salad dressing.

Fill a bottle or wide-mouthed jar with dry nasturtium flowers, shaken free of insects. Add a few peeled shallots and a few cloves of garlic. Fill it up with vinegar, cap, and let it stand for 2 or 3 months. Then strain and add salt, cayenne pepper and soy sauce to taste. Bottle and cap securely. (Empty sauce bottles with plastic shaker tops, washed and dried, are perfect to use. Soak the plastic tops in a weak solution of bleach and water to remove traces of the previous sauce.)

II
SWEET

Flower Fritters
Candied Flowers
Rhubarb and Rose Petal Jam
Rhubarb and Elder Flower Jam
Cherry and Rose Conserve
Rose Omelette Soufflé
Rose Petal Jam
Rose Water-Ice
Rose Hip Soup
Primrose Tart
Rose Mousse
Rose Petal Cambrosia
Creole Orange Flower and Rose Conserve
A Dish of Pomegranates
Muscatel Syrup
Rose Junket
White Chocolate and Violet Mousse

FLOWER FRITTERS

Lilac, fruit blossoms, mimosa, elder flowers, acacia and squash flowers make delicious, delicate fritters. The taste is fleeting but the shapes and textures are lovely. They must be cooked and served immediately as they will become soggy if left more than a few minutes. Someone other than the cook should deliver them to the table. The flowers must be picked on a dry, sunny day. They will not cook properly if they are damp. The subtle flavour of the flowers is obscured by anything other than the plainest batter.

> 1 teacup plain or self-raising flour; 3 tablespoons light vegetable oil; approx. 1 teacup cold water; oil for cooking; sugar or salt.

Put the flour into a mixing bowl and add the oil gradually, stirring to blend. Slowly add the water, stirring constantly until the mixture is the consistency of thin cream. Add a pinch of salt if you are cooking zucchini (courgette) flowers.

Pour about 3 inches of light vegetable oil into a deep frying pan and heat it until it is just about to smoke. Quickly dip the flowers into the batter, coating them completely, and drop them into the hot oil. They should puff up and begin to brown right away. Remove with a slotted spoon and leave to drain for a few seconds on paper towels. Sprinkle with sugar or salt and serve immediately.

CANDIED FLOWERS

Delicate crystallized flowers are beautiful decorations for puddings, ice cream, cakes, fruit salads or just to crunch on their own while sipping a comforting tisane or a flower ratafia while reading a romantic novel or a love letter. Use tiny rose buds, pinks, rose petals, violets, mimosa, lilacs, cowslips, fruit or herb flowers and mint leaves. It must be done on a very dry day. Pick the flowers, remove all stems and green, trim the white heels from rose petals and pinks. Wash and dry them thoroughly. There are several methods:

1)   Beat 2 or more egg whites until frothy. Paint each flower, leaf or petal with the egg white with a clean, soft paint brush, then hold with tweezers and dip each one into sugar and make sure that they are completely coated. Place on a baking sheet or tray and dry them in an airing cupboard or warm oven with the door ajar.

2) Beat egg white until frothy and then add enough icing sugar to make a soft, coating paste. Apply with a brush, then place each flower on a tray or baking sheet and sprinkle with sugar. Dry as above.

3) Dissolve 2 ounces of gum arabic (sold in Oriental stores as Goonder or Edible Gum) in 10 ounces of rose water. You may need to heat it gently. Allow to cool, then dip each flower into the mixture and then into sugar. Dry as above.

4) Place 1 cup of sugar and $\frac{1}{2}$ cup of water and a pinch of cream of tartar in a saucepan. Cook over a fairly high heat, stirring with a wooden spoon until it forms a syrup and spins a thread off the spoon. Dip each flower into the syrup and then dip or sprinkle with sugar. Dry as above.

When all your flowers are dry, place them between sheets of waxed or greaseproof paper in boxes or tins.

RHUBARB AND
ROSE PETAL JAM

Jam making is one of the many things that become easier with experience. The tendency at first, for me anyway, was to over-boil and caramelize the sugar, which doesn't quite spoil the jam but does ruin the colour. You have to watch it very carefully as it boils and be sure to take the pan off the heat while you test for a set.

Before you start, put a saucer into the refrigerator and when you want to test the boiling jam, put a few drops on to the cool plate, wait a few seconds and then push it with your finger. When it wrinkles up it is ready. When you can smell the sugar it is too late; but just before that happens it makes a sort of crackling sound. That should mean it is just about right. Whip it off the heat and test.

This rhubarb and rose petal jam is lovely on its own but is also a good filling for baked apples or a sweet omelette. I have used dried rose buds for making it. When using them, rub off the green and shake to extract the seeds. Use only the petals.

> 1 lb rhubarb, cut into half-inch pieces; 1 lb sugar; juice of 1 lemon; 2 handfuls of fresh rose petals or 5 roses (white heels discarded, petals cut into strips) or 2 handfuls of dried rose petals or buds (as directed above).

Cover the rhubarb with the sugar and lemon juice and leave to stand overnight. Add the rose petals to the rhubarb mixture and place in a large, heavy saucepan. Cook over a brisk heat, stirring until the sugar is dissolved, and boil until it sets. Cool it slightly and pour into clean, warm, dry jars and seal with waxed discs and cellophane, melted wax, or a quarter-inch layer of sugar, and cover.

RHUBARB AND
ELDER FLOWER JAM

As a change from the more usual combination of elder flower and gooseberries, I have adapted this from *The Country Housewife's Handbook* published by the West Kent Federation of Women's Institutes in 1939.

> 1 lb rhubarb, cut into 2-inch lengths; 3 heads of elder flower, tied in a muslin bag; 1 lb sugar; juice and grated rind of 1 lemon.

Put the rhubarb in a mixing bowl with the elder flower bag buried in the middle. Stir in the sugar. Cover and leave for 24 hours, stirring it after 12 hours. The next day heat the mixture in a large heavy saucepan but do not boil. Pour back into the bowl and leave for another 24 hours. Then remove the elder flowers, add the juice and lemon rind to the rhubarb. Boil until it sets. Pot and seal.

Try this instead of rose jam with the omelette soufflé on page 47.

CHERRY AND ROSE CONSERVE

Cherries and roses are a lovely combination. Use any strongly scented roses; the cherries will give it a beautiful deep ruby colour. Cherries can be pitted with a cherry-pitter, available at an ironmonger or good department or hardware store. I don't mind them not being whole and squeeze the pits out with my fingers, over the saucepan so as not to lose any of the juice.

> 1 lb cherries (sour if you can get them), pitted; ¾ lb sugar; 5 fragrant roses, rinsed and shaken dry (snip off the white heels, discard them, and cut the petals into strips); juice of half a lemon.

Combine all of the ingredients in a heavy saucepan. Cook over a fairly brisk heat and stir until the sugar is dissolved. Bring to the boil and continue cooking, stirring occasionally, for about 20 minutes until the mixture has thickened. Let it cool, then pour into clean, warm jars and seal.

ROSE OMELETTE SOUFFLÉ

An omelette soufflé requires the same number of eggs and the same amount of butter as fried eggs but shows more respect and is an elegant finale to a light supper. It is sound advice, given to me many years ago, to try out a new dish for yourself before serving it to guests.

> 6 eggs, separated; 6 tablespoons sugar; 1 tablespoon orange flower water; rose jam to cover the bottom of a buttered 7-inch soufflé dish.

Preheat the oven to 425°F/Gas No. 7. Cream the egg yolks with the sugar and orange flower water in a mixing bowl until they are smooth and creamy and the sugar is dissolved. Whip the egg whites until very stiff and carefully fold into the egg yolk and sugar mixture. Pour on to the jam in the soufflé dish and bake for about 15 minutes. Serve immediately.

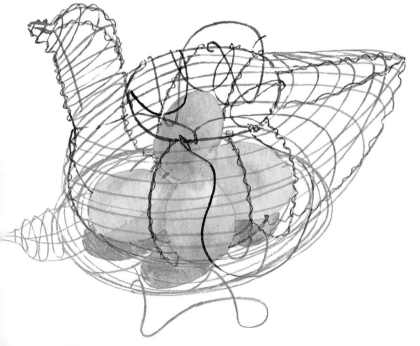

ROSE PETAL JAM

The learned and passionate lover of flowers Eleanour Sinclair Rohde wrote that this is 'a confection fit for Titania and should be served in the daintiest jars'. How right she was, rose jam is sublime. Ideally the roses used should be deep in colour and richly scented. If you have to use paler roses, the colour can be improved with a few drops of red food colouring. It should look as delicious as it is. It makes exquisite tiny sandwiches for a special tea or as the base for a beautiful water-ice, or melted as a sweet sauce for custard or pudding.

> 1 lb fresh rose petals, the white part cut off; 1 pint water; 1 lb sugar; juice of 2 lemons; 2–3 teaspoons of rose water and (if needed) a few drops of red food colouring.

Rinse the petals and leave them to drain. Simmer in the water for a few minutes until tender in a heavy saucepan. (Make sure it is big enough for the sugar to foam up, only fill it half full.) Add the sugar and lemon juice and cook over a brisk heat, stirring until the sugar is dissolved and begins to thicken. When it is bubbling up nicely (the bubbles will go from large to smaller) begin to test for a set. Don't worry about getting it solid, it should be slightly runny. Let it cool down and then pour while still warm into warmed, sterilized jars. Seal with waxed discs or a layer of sugar and cover.

ROSE WATER-ICE

Even people who are always dieting will usually succumb to the temptation of a water-ice. It looks so much less fattening than it actually is. It is possible to get the light, fluffy texture of what Italians call *semi-freddo* or what English-speaking people usually call Mr Softee or Tastee Freez by whipping it when half frozen. If your jam is not very red you will probably want to use food colouring to tint the ice a pretty pink. It is absolutely delicious and looks superb. Decorate each serving with candied rose petals if you have any.

$1\frac{1}{2}$ pints water; $\frac{1}{2}$ lb white sugar; 3 tablespoons rose petal jam; red food colouring.

Put the water and sugar into a heavy saucepan. Bring to the boil, stirring until the sugar is dissolved. Add the jam and boil until it becomes syrupy – about the thickness of the syrup in tinned fruit. Allow to cool and then pour into a container to freeze. A metal bowl is perfect. When it is just about frozen, remove and whip it to a froth (in a food processor if you have one), adding food colouring until the colour is right. Put back into the freezer until ready to serve. If you haven't made your own, you can buy rose jam and other flower jams in Oriental shops or fancy food stores.

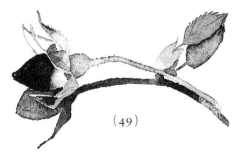

(49)

ROSE HIP SOUP

There is no reason why soup should always be served at the beginning of a meal. The Chinese often serve a hot soup in the middle of a banquet and a cold sweet soup at the end. In Sweden rose hip soup is so popular it is sold in tins in every grocers and is served at the end of a meal. Rose hips are rich in Vitamin C so it is good to have in the winter if fruit is scarce. From *Scandinavian Cookery* by Elizabeth Craig.

'1 lb dried red rose hips; 2 quarts cold water; 6–8 oz sugar; 1 tablespoon cornflour; ½ pint whipped cream [sour cream or *fromage blanc*]; ¼ lb almonds.

'Soak the hips for 12 hours in the water. Turn hips and water into a saucepan. Bring to boil. Simmer gently till into a pulp, stirring occasionally. Strain juice into a saucepan. Add sugar. Bring to boiling point. Cream the cornflour with cold water and stir in. Stir till boiling. Simmer for 3 minutes, stirring constantly. Dish up. Spoon a tablespoon of the cream over each portion, then sprinkle cream lightly with tiny shredded blanched almonds. When the weather is cold, serve soup tepid. When the weather is hot, serve soup chilled.'

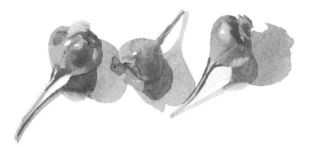

PRIMROSE TART

Primroses, 'the glory of the spring' as Ben Jonson called them, still grow wild in profusion in some parts of the country, and you can grow them from seed. This recipe from *Wild Fruits, Berries, Nuts and Flowers* can also be made with roses and apples, or roses and cherries. The petals may be fresh or dried.

'Line a buttered tart tin with thin pastry. Cover with generous layer of sliced apples and castor sugar. Sprinkle well with yellow primrose petals and then with more castor sugar. Cover with pastry and bake in the usual way.'

In the 1930s there was something of a revival of flower cookery. Almost all of Mrs Leyel's books included recipes using flowers. *Flowers as Food* by Florence White was published in 1934; *Rose Recipes* by Eleanour Sinclair Rohde in 1939. *The Vicomte in the Kitchen*, 1933, by the Vicomte de Maudit has all the sophisticated glamour of the period – the last hectic gasp of euphoria between the great wars. The Vicomte was very fond of roses and claimed to have introduced rose petal jam into English households. Here are two of his sweet dishes using the jam on page 48 and the rose brandy on page 72.

ROSE MOUSSE

'Beat the whites of five eggs to a froth, add by degrees five dessertspoonfuls of rose petal jam. Pour the mixture into a round fireproof dish, add if available one good liqueur glass of rose brandy, and cook over a good fire for five minutes, stirring constantly.'

ROSE PETAL CAMBROSIA

'Rub a small jar of rose petal jam through a sieve, and add three liqueur glasses of rose brandy. Add one pint of whipped cream, mix and place in deep champagne glasses, and serve with a long spoon and biscuits.'

CREOLE ORANGE FLOWER
AND ROSE CONSERVE

The *Picayune Creole Cook Book* (1901) whose pages conjure up the haunting smells of my brief childhood sojourn in New Orleans – strong spices, roasting coffee and the molasses factory – says 'this is a delicious and recherché Creole Conserve'. It is extremely sweet and sticky and is superb on hot scones or toast and also makes an unusual sauce for puddings or ice cream. It should have the consistency of thick honey.

> 2 oz powdered orange flower petals (available dried at good herbalists and can be pulverized in a clean coffee grinder); $1\frac{1}{2}$ lbs white sugar; 8 oz rose water.

Steep the petals in a very little distilled or mineral water, then add the sugar to the petals in a saucepan and put over a moderate heat. Add the rose water. Cook until it begins to jell (it will never set firm) and turn into small glass jars. Cover and store until needed.

A DISH OF POMEGRANATES

Food in Europe has never been the same since the Crusaders first tasted sugar, almonds, pistachios, dates, pomegranates and rose water in the Holy Lands. Between 1096 and 1291 these exotic foods were brought back home and introduced into the cuisine of northern Europe. Food in the 'Saracen style' became *à la mode*. Three of these ingredients are combined in this elegantly simple dish from Elizabeth David's *A Book of Mediterranean Food*. It is important that it be perfectly chilled which is why Mrs David suggests using a silver bowl. It looks very beautiful in glass, like a dish of Oriental rubies, and is wonderfully tart and refreshing.

'Take all the insides from 6 pomegranates and mash them into a silver bowl. Sprinkle with rose water, lemon juice and sugar and serve iced.'

Look for pomegranates which are plump, smooth and shiny. Cut them in half and squeeze them into your dish. Pick out the bitter white membrane which separates the seeds. Add the sugar and rose water with caution. It should not be overly sweet nor should the rose water dominate, but only delicately perfume the fruit.

MUSCATEL SYRUP

It is hard for those of us who cannot remember rationing to imagine how frustrating it must have been to try and cook with hardly any sugar, cream or citrus fruit; no imported wines, liqueurs, vanilla beans or rubber gloves. Constance Spry in her wartime book *Come into the Garden, Cook* (1942) rather wistfully recalls strawberries with orange juice, liqueurs or thick cream but says that nothing is really much better with them than muscatel syrup, and that strawberry jam made with sugar, currant juice instead of water and flavoured with elder flowers is 'something quite out of the ordinary'.

2 lbs sugar; $\frac{1}{2}$ pint water; 2 lbs green gooseberries; 8–10 heads of elder flowers, washed but left on their stalks.

Melt the sugar in the water over a brisk heat, stirring until the sugar is dissolved. Add the cleaned gooseberries and elder flowers. Simmer without breaking the fruit. When the fruit is cooked, strain, cool and bottle.

'This mixture makes an exquisite syrup with a flavour like muscatel, and is delicious with water or soda water. This syrup keeps a short time, but it is worth while to put some of it into jars, and to sterilize it as you would fruit so that you have supplies over a longer period.'

ROSE JUNKET

Junket and tapioca pudding are foods those of us of a certain age remember from childhood. Adults either love or loathe them. Elisabeth Ayrton wrote in *The Cookery of England* that 'junket was the most common festive sweet dish from the Middle Ages to the eighteenth century. It was served on holidays, at feasts and fairs so universally that they were often called "junket-days" and people spoke of going "a-junketing".'

> 1 pint milk; pinch mace and cinnamon; 1 teaspoon rennet; 2 tablespoons sugar; 1–2 tablespoons rose water or rose brandy; few drops red or pink food colouring; freshly grated nutmeg.

Warm the milk just to blood heat, stir in the spices, rennet, sugar, rose water or brandy and food colouring. It is greatly improved by being coloured pale pink. Leave to set in a moderately cool place, not the refrigerator, in a wide shallow dish or in individual dishes or stemmed glasses, and sprinkle lightly with nutmeg. Serve covered with cream flavoured with rose water and dusted with sugar. Surround with deep damask rose petals or candied rose petals if you have any.

(57)

WHITE CHOCOLATE AND VIOLET MOUSSE

White chocolate is wickedly rich. Dark chocolate mousse is splendid, especially when made with extra bitter chocolate and orange flower water, but this one is deliciously unctuous and dense. It does need alcohol to cut the sweetness a little. I make it with home-made violet liqueur or vanilla brandy. If you want a stronger scent of violets add a teaspoonful of violet flavouring with brandy, rum or any liqueur.

> 5 oz white chocolate (1 large Milky Bar); 2 eggs; 1–2 tablespoons spirit; 10 oz double cream; candied violets.

Break the chocolate into small pieces. Put them into a blender with the eggs, spirit and flavouring. Blend until smooth. Add the cream and blend for a minute or two more. Pour into small glasses or *demi-tasses* (these quantities will fill 6) to chill. Decorate with candied violets just before serving.

Variation: Use single cream and freeze in a metal bowl. Whip into a froth (in a food processor if you have one) before serving. The violets look very pretty in their mounds of 'snow'.

III
SPIRITUOUS

Hydromel

Maraschino

Rose Petal Punch

Borage in Wine:

Victorian Claret Cup

Claret Cup II

Rosemary Wine

Ratafia of Carnations,

Violets or Orange Blossoms

Gold Water

Perkam Bitter

May Brandy

Hawthorn Cocktail

Rose Liqueur Brandy

Elder Flower 'Champagne'

Violet Liqueur

Vicomte's Cocktail

Pamela Cocktail

Vicomte's Cup

Thistle Punch

HYDROMEL

'Hydromel' means honey-water and was the Greek name the Latins used for mead. Honey was the only sweetener for food and drink before sugar arrived from the East. Mead was the drink of Celt and Saxon warriors and nobles – the great hall of a Saxon palace was called the mead hall. Although wine was introduced after the Norman Conquest and ale was still the most popular drink, mead and metheglin were revived after the Restoration and became fashionable among the gentry. When Sir Kenelm Digby was gathering recipes for *The Closet Opened* (1669) he collected 56 different versions of honey-based liqueurs from his friends.

> 1 oz elder flowers, picked as they just begin to open, leaves and stalks removed; ½ oz orris root powder (the ground root of *Iris florentina* which smells of violets, available from a herb shop or good chemist); 1 oz crushed almonds; 1 cup brandy; 3½ oz honey; 1 quart water.

Steep the elder flowers, orris root and almonds in the brandy for 3 days. Dissolve the honey in the warmed water and add the brandy-herb mixture. Filter, cover and leave in a warm place for 2 weeks. Then filter again and rebottle. Serve in tiny glasses as an after-dinner cordial or use as a flavouring for whipped cream or dessert sauces.

MARASCHINO

There are many recipes for maraschino. This version is adapted from one given in *Herb-Lore for Housewives* by C. Romanné-James published in 1938, which says 'maraschino has a very professional sound, but it was a favourite liqueur in old times and is very easy to make'.

1½ lbs Morello cherries; ½ lb peach or cherry leaves; petals of 4 fragrant roses, white heels removed; handful of jasmine flowers (fresh or dried); 1 lb preserving sugar; 1 quart of vodka or brandy.

Pit the cherries over a large jar, do not waste any of the juice. Crack the stones and add the kernels to the cherries. Add the peach or cherry leaves. Lightly bruise the flowers in your hands but do not squash them. Put them and the sugar and spirit into the jar, cover, and let it stand for a month. Then strain carefully through a paper coffee filter and rebottle. Store in a cool dark place. It will improve with age.

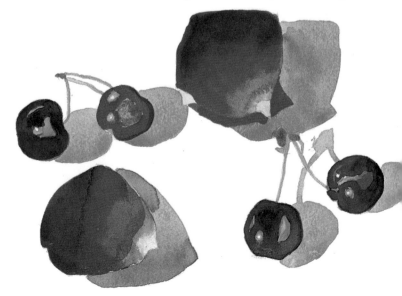

ROSE PETAL PUNCH

A handful of strongly-scented rose petals will delicately flavour a punch for a summer evening.

Two or three hours before you want to serve the punch put a good handful of fresh, scented rose petals into a mixing bowl. Sprinkle a tablespoon of sugar over the roses and pour over it a large bottle of sparkling water and the juice of 1 lemon. Chill. When ready to serve, strain off the liquid into a punch bowl and add a bottle of red or chilled white wine. Serve in tall glasses.

BORAGE IN WINE

'The sprigs of borage in wine are of known virtue to revive the hypochondriac and cheer the hard student,' wrote John Evelyn in *Acetaria* in 1699. It was listed as one of the four cordial flowers, with rose, violet and bugloss in the *Household Companion* of Dr Salmon in 1710 and is said to be the famous nepenthe of Homer, 'of such rare virtue that when drunk steep'd in wine, if wife, and children, father and mother, brother and sister, and all thy dearest friends should die before thy face, thou couldst not grieve, or shed a tear for them'. John Gerard's 1597 herbal quoted both Pliny and Dioscorides affirming that borage 'maketh a man merry and joyful'. Today it cheers almost exclusively in Pimm's but our ancestors would have been more likely to use it in a claret cup, finding it, as Dr Fernie wrote, almost as 'beneficial as a bracing sojourn by the seaside during an autumn holiday.'

VICTORIAN CLARET CUP

Dissolve 1 large teaspoon of white sugar in a little hot water in a punch bowl. Add 1 glass of sherry, half a glass of brandy, half a glass of maraschino, a thin rind of lemon peel and a strip of cucumber rind. Pour in 1 bottle of claret. Let it stand for an hour. When ready to serve, add ice, a sprig of flowering borage and soda water or a not too strongly flavoured fizzy mineral water. Serve in tall glasses with a few blue borage flowers floating on the top.

CLARET CUP II

1 lemon, sliced very thinly; 1 bottle claret; 2
bottles lemonade; 1 bottle soda water or
sparkling mineral water; 1 wineglass
maraschino; 2 oz sugar; as many sprigs of
borage as there are glasses.

Place the lemon slices in a punch bowl and pour
over the liquid ingredients. Add the sugar and stir
to dissolve. Add ice and serve in tall glasses with a
sprig of flowering borage in each one.

ROSEMARY WINE

According to Dr Fernie, rosemary wine when taken in small quantities is a 'quietening cordial to a weak heart, subject to palpitations' and 'stimulates the kidneys, thus preventing dropsy'. It also 'stimulates the brain and nervous system and proves of service against headaches of a feeble circulation and of languid health'. He also advises that much of the active volatile principle resides in the calices of the flowers, so that they should be retained for storage and use.

Chop half a dozen sprigs of rosemary with their flowering tops into one-inch lengths and place them in a wide-mouthed glass jar. Fill up with white wine. Strain off after 2 or 3 days and rebottle. It can be drunk immediately but will also keep.

RATAFIA OF CARNATIONS, VIOLETS OR ORANGE BLOSSOMS

Alice B. Toklas lived most of her long life in France, where she must have tasted and prepared many delicious home-made liqueurs. She wrote in *Aromas and Flavors* that they are 'useful, economical and little trouble to prepare . . . combining them is always a pleasure, can become a passion, a pastime'. Here is an adaptation of her flower ratafia.

$\frac{1}{2}$ lb of petals of carnations, violets, orange blossoms, stamens and stems removed; 1 clove and 1-inch stick of cinnamon; 1 quart of rectified spirit (rectified ethyl alcohol sold by licensed chemists), vodka or white *eau de vie*.

Place all of the ingredients in a large bottle or glass jar. Cover and leave to infuse for 1 month. Then strain and filter through coffee filters. Add sugar to taste. Rebottle when the sugar has dissolved.

(67)

GOLD WATER

Glittering gold which never tarnishes has long been associated with longevity, and the idea of consuming it to prolong life is ancient. Taoist alchemists in China tried to make gold with sulphur and the red sulphide of mercury known as cinnabar or vermilion – gold and red are the magic colours of alchemy. This alchemical gold did not prolong life when eaten, but had the opposite effect. The Greeks regarded the yellow colour of gold as its vital property. The Arabs, who had contact with both cultures via the trade routes, introduced the concept to the Crusaders, who brought it back home to Europe where a vogue for 'endoring' or colouring food yellow to imitate gold lasted for centuries. At Elizabethan banquets exotic fruits such as pomegranates, oranges, cucumbers and grapes were often spangled with gold. A good art supply shop should be able to provide sheets of gold leaf – real, not alchemical.

> 1 piece of stick cinnamon; 6 whole cloves; 4 mace blades; rind of 1 lemon; 3 teaspoons coriander seed; 2 oz dried orange blossoms (available at a herb shop); 2 leaves gold leaf; 2 pints *eau de vie*, vodka or brandy.

Place all of the dry ingredients (except the gold leaf) in a glass jar or large bottle. Add the spirit and let it infuse for 6 weeks. Then filter through paper coffee filters and add sugar to taste. Shake to dissolve the sugar. Cut the gold leaf into tiny pieces and add to the liqueur. Rebottle. Shake before serving to make sure a little of the gold goes into each glass.

PERKAM BITTER

The Norwegian writer Sigrid Undset, discussing the use of herbs in Norway in the *Herbarist Magazine* in 1945, wrote that her maternal grandfather, who never touched wine or hard liquor except on his birthday and New Year's Day, started every morning of his adult life with a dram of Perkam Bitter. As he enjoyed splendid health until he was eighty-seven and lived to be ninety-three, she thought it probably did him good. She says it is very bitter and may be diluted 'like one does with Angostura and may be introduced with advantage in some kinds of cocktail'.

Gather the flowers and full-blown buds of St John's Wort (*Hypericum perforatum*) and dry them on a tray or basket in the sun. Fill a large glass jar with the dried flowers but do not press them down. Pour aquavit, gin or vodka over the flowers and make sure they are completely covered. The liquid begins to turn pink almost immediately. Cover securely and leave for 3 months, then strain off the liquid which is now a deep garnet colour, filter through muslin, cheesecloth or paper coffee filters and rebottle.

MAY BRANDY

Hawthorn, or May, is like Friday the 13th. Lucky for some, unlucky for others. Its supernatural powers of protection against evil were particularly employed at *bealtaine* – later May Day – the pagan spring rite of sacrifice and purification when fairies and witches were especially active. In Ireland a May tree growing alone is still regarded as the domain of fairies and must not be disturbed. In the summer of 1969 I was living in County Limerick where the scandal of the district was the cutting down in the middle of the night of a fairy tree in a nearby village. There are many who still think it dangerous to bring May into the house. Hawthorn flowers were mentioned as food in the thirteenth century and May brandy goes back at least to the eighteenth century. You can always make it out of doors and it is a lovely soft flavouring for cream, custards and sweet sauces. Some say it is better than the best cherry brandy.

Fill a wide-mouthed jar with May flowers removed from their stems (one way of doing this is to pinch the stem between the thumb and forefinger and clip it with your fingernail), cover with brandy, leave to infuse for 2–3 months, then strain and rebottle. A Scottish cookery book of 1899 suggests using whisky instead of brandy.

HAWTHORN COCKTAIL

'J.V.', writing about 'Nectar from the Hedge-row' in the *Evening News* in the 1930s, gave a recipe for this cocktail quoted by Florence White in *Flowers as Food* in 1934.

1 bottle of still white wine, Sauterne or hock; ½ bottle red Beaune or Chambéry; 1 orange, sliced; sprig of lemon thyme and 2 sprigs of borage; handful of fresh hawthorn flowers. Pour the wine into a bowl, add to it the orange slices, herbs and flowers. Cover it with a tea towel and leave it to stand for a night and a day. Strain and shake with ice in a cocktail shaker or stir with ice in a jug. Decorate the glasses with a sprig of flowering borage or a few borage flowers.

ROSE LIQUEUR BRANDY

The following recipes are from *The Vicomte in the Kitchen* by the Vicomte de Maudit, published in 1933. He had a rather extravagant turn of phrase: 'Now I shall give away my secret of how to make the most delicious liqueur in the world.' He also gives explicit directions on how to pick your roses: 'Pick eight large red roses . . . they should be picked in the early morning before the sun's rays have touched them. The best sorts of roses are: General McArthur, Victory, Richmond, Chateau de Clos Vougeot, Etoile de Hollande, Hugh Dickson, George Dickson, Lady Helen Maglona and especially red Provence . . . Be careful that no previous heavy rains have spotted any of the petals, and if the morning dew is still on them, shake out the pearly tears.'

Soak the petals for one month in a jar containing a quart of good cognac brandy. Cork the jar and 'disturb' it very gently once a week. One month later make a syrup of three teacups of preserving sugar and two teacups of still mineral or distilled water. Boil for 20 minutes over a brisk heat. Add the petals (white heels removed) of a dozen roses which have been dusted with sugar, bring it to the boil again and then simmer with a lid on for an hour, stirring occasionally. Strain the brandy and rose mixture into a large glass jar and then stir in the sugar and rose mixture. Stir well and leave the jar open with a piece of muslin or a tea towel over it until the next day. Pour the finished liqueur into bottles and seal.

ELDER FLOWER 'CHAMPAGNE'

The flowers should be picked at the end of a dry summer day when the flavour will be more fully developed. It will be slightly fizzy and ready to drink in 2 months.

> 1 gallon water; 1½ lbs sugar; 7 large heads of elder flower; 1 lemon and 1 orange, sliced; 2 tablespoons white wine vinegar.

Boil the water and pour it over the sugar. When it is cold, add the elder flowers, lemon, orange and vinegar. Cover with a thick cloth and leave for 24 hours. Squeeze the flowers and strain the liquid through a fine sieve or muslin. Store in glass containers – bottles with snap-on tops or glass jars with a hinged lid and a rubber seal. Serve iced.

VIOLET LIQUEUR

'Of all the fragrant herbs I send, none can compare in nobleness with the purple violet,' wrote the medieval Bishop of Poitiers, Venatus Fortunatus, who was known as the 'Abbé Gastronome'. Violets are, I think, the most romantic of all flowers. The liqueur *Parfait d'Amour* is flavoured with them. There is nothing more enchanting than the scent of wild violets damp with rain, but the heady Parma violet if you grow it is best for this recipe. I have used florist's bunches for it; they are helped by the orris root. It is very good for a head cold (or a hangover – the Romans thought violets helped to dispel the fumes of alcohol) and is a good flavouring for sweet dishes such as the junket on page 57 or the white chocolate mousse on page 58.

> 1 small bottle (approx. 12 oz) of brandy; 10 whole cloves; 1-inch piece of stick cinnamon; 1 piece star anise; 40 violets or 3 florist's bunches, stems and green removed; 3 heaped teaspoons orris root; rind of 1 orange, peeled off in a thin strip with a potato peeler; half a vanilla bean (the pod of a Mexican jungle orchid).

Steep all of the ingredients in the brandy for a month. Add sugar to taste and when it has dissolved filter and add violet food colouring if you want it purple, then rebottle.

VICOMTE'S COCKTAIL

Put some ice in a jug and pour into it one-third gin, one-third French vermouth, and one-third rose brandy. Stir with a glass rod, strain into cocktail glasses and serve with a candied rose petal floating on the top.

PAMELA COCKTAIL

One-third each of gin, Kümmel and rose brandy prepared as above.

VICOMTE'S CUP

2 lemons, sliced; 2 apples, sliced; $\frac{1}{2}$ lb sugar; 6 cloves; 2 leaves of sweet marjoram; 2 leaves tarragon; 2 tablespoons orange flower water; 1 pint Chablis or any good white wine.

Place all of the ingredients in a bowl. Allow to stand for 2 hours, stirring occasionally. Strain the mixture into a punch bowl or jug and chill for 20 minutes before serving.

THISTLE PUNCH

Dried thistle heads are usually to be found in the
countryside throughout the autumn and winter.
Serve this on any occasion with a Scottish connec-
tion.

> 5 slices of lemon; 5 leaves of tarragon; 5
> cloves; 1 tumbler of Italian vermouth; 3
> tumblers of whisky; 10 thistle heads; 1½ pints
> of water.

Place the lemon, tarragon, cloves, vermouth and
whisky in a bowl and set aside. Remove the outer
husks from 5 of the thistles and boil the kernels in
the water. Simmer for 10 minutes. Then pour the
water and the kernels into the whisky mixture,
decorate with the remaining 5 thistles and heat
gently in a saucepan or *bain marie* before serving.

IV
TEAS AND
TISANES

Nosegay Tea
Tea for the Blues
Tisane of Four Flowers
Kahwah Beida
Thyme Tea and Conserve

NOSEGAY TEA

Use a good black China tea such as Oolong,
Keemun or Orange Pekoe whose flavour is delicately flowery (tea is made from the leaves of
Camellia sinensis) rather than an Earl Grey or
Lapsang Souchong whose rich smokiness is too
powerful for the subtle flower tastes. Violet tea is
recommended for bronchitis, fever and what a
five-year-old friend of mine calls 'guitar'.

   1 measure each of dried or fresh violets,
   jasmine, rose buds or petals and black China
   tea.

Mix together with your hands in a bowl. Store in
air-tight tins. Use one or two heaped tablespoons
per pot and drink without milk. A very small
amount of sugar or honey will enhance the flavour
if you like sweet tea.

TEA FOR THE BLUES

For those tenebrous days when you're singing the 'I've Got the You Don't Know the Half of It Dearie Blues'. The slightly peppery sharpness of the lavender will help a headache and the warm honey of the orange flowers and soothing lemon verbena will calm jangled nerves.

> 1 measure lemon verbena; 1 measure dried orange blossoms; $\frac{1}{2}$ measure dried lavender.

Mix together in a bowl with your hands. Store in air-tight tins. Use 1 or 2 heaped tablespoons per pot and drink without milk.

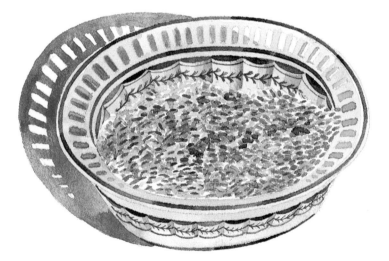

TISANE OF FOUR FLOWERS

From *A Garden of Herbs* by Eleanour Sinclair Rohde.

'Lime flowers, orange flowers, borage and camomile. Half a pint of boiling water poured on to a heaped dessertspoon of these dried flowers.

'In spite of its name *tisane de quatre fleurs* has sometimes more ingredients. Dried violets, for instance, are frequently added.'

Use equal measures of each of the 4 or 5 flowers. Store away from heat and light.

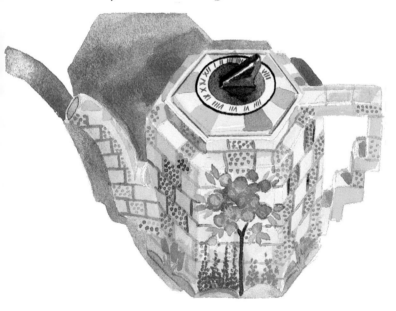

KAHWAH BEIDA
(White Coffee)

This is said to be effective against sleeplessness. It is very popular in Lebanon where I first enjoyed it. In elegant households and smart restaurants a silver ewer of orange flower water is passed around with sugar and tiny glasses in silver holders. You can prepare it yourself or let each guest add *eau de fleurs* and sugar to their own taste.

Fill each glass or *demi-tasse* with hot water and a teaspoon each of white sugar and orange flower water. Stir to dissolve the sugar.

(84)

THYME TEA AND CONSERVE

Dr Fernie wrote in *Meals Medicinal* that thyme tea 'is good against nervous headache, hysterical troubles, flatulence and the headache which follows inebriation'. He also recommends a conserve made from the flowers and leaves of thyme for those 'troubled with the falling sickness'.

For the tea, pour boiling water over a teaspoon of thyme flowers or a few sprigs of dried or fresh thyme in a cup.

For the conserve pound or process the flowering tops of thyme with an equal amount of sugar and keep in small covered pots. This can be dissolved in a cup of hot water or taken neat a spoonful at a time.

SCENTED FLOWERS FOR
MODERN GARDENERS

'What more delightsome than an infinite variety of
sweet smelling flowers? decking with sundry
colours the greene mantle of the earth, the universal
Mother of us all, so by them bespotted, so dyed that
all the world cannot sample them, and wherein it is
more fit to admire the Dyer, than imitate his
workemanship. Colouring not only the Earth but
decking the ayre, and sweetening every breath and
spirit. The Rose red, Damask, Velvet and double
Province rose, the sweet Musk-Rose double and
single, the double and single white Rose; The fair
and sweet scenting Woodbine, the Violet nothing
behind the best for smelling sweetly. A thousand
more will provoke your content.'

William Lawson, *New Orchard and Garden*,
1618

The APOTHECARY Rose

ROSES

Roses more than other flowers have been used for medicine, cosmetics and food. 'Roses do comfort the heart,' wrote William Langham in the sixteenth century. Many roses grown today are of great antiquity. According to Eleanour Sinclair Rohde the Provençal rose, or old cabbage rose, is among the most ancient of garden roses. It may be the 'many petalled rose' of Homer. Pliny mentioned it and also said that 'the isle of Albion is so called from its white cliffs washed by the sea, or from the white roses with which it abounds'. In his time meat was often served covered with fragrant rose petals. Among the most strongly scented would have been the Damask rose which gave its name to the city of Damascus, where they are still grown. The Romans probably introduced the Gallic rose of southern Europe to Britain for culinary purposes along with the garden poppy. Apicius gives a recipe for a *patina* of brains cooked with roses.

Rose water which originally was brought from the East became the fashionable flavouring in Tudor and Stuart England. Spoons were not in regular use until the sixteenth century – forks not until a century later. People still ate with their fingers and the refined expected to be able to wash their hands several times during an elaborate meal. 'Let one attend him with a silver basin/Full of Rose water and bestrewed with flowers' wrote Shakespeare in *The Taming of the Shrew*.

I am indebted to Peter Beales of Intwood Nurseries who specializes in old roses for this list of those which in his expert opinion are the best for cooking.

Gallica: R. g. officinalis 'The Apothecary Rose', Cardinal de Richelieu.
Centifolia: Chapeau de Napoleon, Common Moss, Muscosa, Bullata.
Damask: Kazanlik (especially good), Quatre Saisons.
Bourbon: Mme Isaac Pereire.
Rugosa: Parfum de l'Hay, Roseraie de l'Hay.
Hybrid Perpetual: Dupuy Jamain, Gloire de Ducher, Hugh Dickson and the climber Souvenir du Docteur Jamain.

See also the Vicomte de Maudit's list on page 72.

MARIGOLDS

The cheerful marigold has been known as 'poor man's saffron' and is also said to keep insects away from other plants. The sixteenth-century herbalist William Turner wrote primly, 'Summe use marigolds to make theyr here yellow with the floure of this herbe, not beying content with the naturall colour which God hath geven them.' The old pot marigold is *Calendula officinalis* and a good modern variety is *C. mandarin*. Sow the seeds in early spring; they will flower after 2 months and will seed themselves again each year.

VIOLETS

If you can harvest them for cooking before the rabbits eat them, it would be wise to plant sweet scented *Viola odorata* or *V. cornuta* and Parma violets. For excellent advice on growing violets see *A Modern Herbal* by Mrs M. Grieve published in paperback by Penguin and in hardback by Jonathan Cape.

PINKS

William Lawson was very fond of pinks and called them 'the King of flowers except the rose ...' *Dianthus caryophyllus* are the gilly flowers of old recipe books, called in French *giroflier* because of their clove scent. Search through seed catalogues for mention of strongly scented varieties, pester your local nursery and gardening friends to look out for some of the older ones, such as Fenbows Nutmeg Clove, Sops-in-Wine, Caesar's Mantle, Old Man's Head, Dickers Clove, Brookham Perfume, Chelsea Pink, Rose de Mai, Mrs Sinkins, and Loveliness.

Other plants with scented flowers that can be used for cooking are: lilac, jasmine, acacia, lavender, nasturtium and scented-leaved geraniums. Herbs which are also useful for their flowers are chives, rosemary, hyssop, borage, thyme, tansy, southernwood and wormwood. There are dozens of good books available on growing and using herbs and most nurseries or seed suppliers have a good selection and many have a mail order service.

Recommended reading: *The Scented Garden*, Rosemary Verey; *The Scented Garden*, Eleanour Sinclair Rohde; *The Fragrant Garden*, Kay N. Sanecki; *Scented Flora of the World* and *Growing Old Fashioned Flowers*, Roy Genders, and anything by Gertrude Jekyll or V. Sackville-West.

SOURCES
MENTIONED
IN THE TEXT

Apicius, *The Roman Cookery Book – The Art of Cooking*, Trans. Barbara Flower & Elisabeth Rosenbaum (1958), Harrap, London 1978

Ayrton, Elisabeth, *The Cookery of England,* André Deutsch, London 1974; Penguin 1977

Boulestin, Marcel, *Simple French Cooking for English Homes* (1923), Heinemann, London 1930

Byron, May, *Pot Luck*, Hodder and Stoughton, London 1932

Craig, Elizabeth, *Court Favourites*, André Deutsch, London 1953; *Scandinavian Cookery*, André Deutsch, London 1958

David, Elizabeth, *A Book of Mediterranean Food* (1950), *Elizabeth David Classics*, Jill Norman, London 1980

Digby, Sir Kenelm, *The Closet of the Eminently Learned Sir Kenelm Digby, Knight, Opened* (1669), Ed. Anne Macdonnell, Philip Lee Warner, London 1910

Evelyn, John, *Acetaria – A Discourse of Sallets* (1699), Prospect Books facsimile, London 1982

Fernie, Dr W. T., *Meals Medicinal*, John Wright, Bristol 1905

Hartley, Dorothy, *Food in England* (1954), Macdonald, London 1979

James, B., *Wild Fruits, Berries, Nuts and Flowers – 101 Good Recipes for Using Them*, Medici Society, London 1942

Johnston, Mireille, *The Cuisine of the Sun* (1976), Vintage Books, New York 1979

Leyel, Mrs C. F., *Green Salads and Fruit Salads*, Routledge, London 1925; *Picnics for Motorists*, Routledge, London 1936

Maudit, the Vicomte de, *The Vicomte in the Kitchen* (1933), Clarke, London 1937

Rohde, Eleanour Sinclair, *A Garden Of Herbs* (1936), Dover, New York 1969; *Rose Recipes* (1939), Dover, New York 1973

Romanné-James, C., *Herb-Lore for Housewives*, Herbert Jenkins, London 1938

Spry, Constance, *Come into the Garden, Cook* (1942), Dent, London 1952

Toklas, Alice B. (with Poppy Cannon), *Aromas and Flavors of Past and Present*, Harper, New York 1958

Warner, Rev. Richard, *Antiquitates Culinariae* (*The Forme of Cury*) (1791), Prospect Books facsimile, London 1981

White, Florence, *Flowers as Food*, Jonathan Cape, London 1934; *Good Things in England*, Jonathan Cape, London 1932

Weights and Measures

Liquid

1 pint = 20 fl oz (16 fl oz American)
$$= 2 \text{ cups} = 4.7 \text{ dl}$$
½ pint = 10 fl oz (8 fl oz American)
$$= 1 \text{ cup} = 2.4 \text{ dl}$$
¼ pint = 5 fl oz (4 fl oz American)
$$= \tfrac{1}{2} \text{ cup} = 1.2 \text{ dl}$$

1 litre = 35.7 fl oz
½ litre = 17.5 fl oz

Dry

1 lb = 16 oz = 450 g
½ lb = 8 oz = 225 g
¼ lb = 4 oz = 110 g
1 oz = 25 g

INDEX